Glimpses
of
Grace

Poems for Life

Brenda Wheaton Diffin

Brenda Wheaton Diffin

Copyright ©2021 Brenda Wheaton Diffin

All rights reserved. No part of this publication may be reproduced, distributed, or transmitted in any form or by any means, including photocopying, recording, or other electronic or mechanical methods, without the prior written permission of the publisher, except in the case of brief quotations embodied in critical reviews and certain other noncommercial uses permitted by copyright law.

Tyndale House Publishers. 2004. Holy Bible: New Living Translation. Wheaton, Ill: Tyndale House Publishers. All rights reserved.

Scripture taken from the New King James Version®. Copyright © 1982 by Thomas Nelson. Used by permission. All rights reserved.

Publishers.ISBN-978-1-951300-24-1

Liberation's Publishing – West Point - Mississippi

Dedicated to family and friends who have shared in the victories of the journey and also, in the consequences.

Thank you for your love.

Table of Contents

- Introduction 7
- His Child 11
- Born Again 13
- His Chosen Vessel 15
- Windswept 17
- Prayer 19
- Time 19
- Guided 21
- Hold Me 23
- Know Love 25
- Be Love 29
- On Flying 31
- False Bravado 33
- Truth 33

- ❖ A Plan 35
- ❖ Why Christmas 37
- ❖ Beside Still Waters 41
- ❖ Out of Darkness 44
- ❖ Inside Story 47
- ❖ Companionship 49
- ❖ Don't Cry 51
- ❖ Reflections 53
- ❖ Christ is Dawn 55
- ❖ Possibility 57
- ❖ Peace 59

Introduction

Now, first of all, let me say that I am not a poet. I do love reading and I love words but could not have put these poems together without Divine help. As the Psalmist has said, "My help cometh from the Lord."

I would like these writings to show the incredible Grace of God and the way He speaks to us by His Written Word, the Holy Bible, and by His Spirit who whispers to our hearts just in the way the Word fits us, as individuals. Thus, for me, the poems. They rhyme, so they are easy to remember; they are simple, everyday words so could be sung, and they are so full of promise and faith, they have encouraged me year after year. They have come to me over and over at times when I needed them sleeping and waking and once even under sedation. They have stood the tests of my life and the tests of time even as the scriptures they come from.

The journey, for me, has been surely and completely full of grace. I am not special. I am just a seeker after God, His truth and hope. He has done all the leading, answering and blessing of favor that was unmerited on my part. His love encompasses me, covers me, and fills my life in good times and bad. The reason I share these poems is that they came from Him. They are real in a world of real hurt, pain, and loss. Since they all point back to Him, I would like my children and grandchildren to have them as part of their heritage from Him. They were given to me, but not just for me.

I was taught at a young age that Jesus loves me. I was taught the Ten Commandments and knew the stories of the Bible heroes and heroines: Moses, Samson, Joshua, David, Abraham, Joseph, Esther, Jacob, Mary, and more. I married at 19 and had three wonderful children by age 26. We were not in church. I would have called myself a Christian. But I had no relationship with God or Jesus, the Christ, (Messiah, Promised One.)

The poems begin my journey at around this time. We were living in Long Island, New York when my heart was stirred to know Him. We moved soon to Alexandria, Virginia, and the awakening continued. The years were mostly the 1970s. I am putting this together in 2021 out of obedience to the prompting of the Holy Spirit.

So, let's begin here.

Glimpses of Grace

I had been taught that Jesus is the Good Shepherd. And though it is true that I have at times been a wandering sheep, it is also true that I am His child. I was reading Romans in The Living Bible and the words leaped out at me that I was truly a child of God. In Chapter 8, Verse 16, it reads,

"For His Holy Spirit speaks to us deep in our hearts and tells us that we really are God's Children." **Romans 8:16 (NLT)**

"His Child" came from that profound revelation deep within me.

His Child

The Father spoke and said to me
Oh, listen very carefully
Know My voice, that within thee
Every joy may be set free
And you may claim eternally
You are My child.

His Voice was strong and very sure
But gentle too, its timbre pure.
He knew my heart was sad and sore
For He had sought me out before.
You will be Mine forever more.
You are My child.

My face was warm and washed with tears
His loving touch dissolved my fears.
I'll gladly give Him all my years
To hear Him as His presence nears
And know Him as each shadow clears.
You are — you are My child.

The next poem, "Born Again", was given to my understanding as my heritage from my mother and grandmother. His Spirit spoke to my heart as He named me "Joy." Joy as action, arms flung wide and even dancing. The Spirit showed me that my mother, who was often a bundle of nerves if not abiding in Him, was truly named "Calm" in Him. My grandmother was named "Trust" as I had never known her when not abiding in Him. Born in Christ, we are made new. Jesus said, "My peace I give to you — not as the world gives." His peace flows as a "Calm" river through the dry lands of life. His peace sown as a prayer and watered by "Trust" brings forth the flower and fruit of "Joy."

Joy, born of a calm trust in Jesus as I abide in Him.

Jesus replied, "What I am telling you so earnestly is this: Unless one is born of water and the Spirit, he cannot enter the Kingdom of God. Men can only reproduce human life, but the Holy Spirit gives new life from heaven." **John 3:5-6 (TLB)**

Born Again

They tell me joy is the daughter of calm
And calm born of trust in One
Whose name is God the Father —
Through Jesus Christ the Son.

My lineage is far less sure
And surely far less grand.
Born of water, born of blood
And born of humble man.

Born in pain and born to cry,
Born to well know sorrow.
Born to grow up wounded,
With questions of the morrow.

But Jesus said "Be born again.
Come join My family tree.
My Father says you are His child
Your Brother I will be."

And that by trusting in His Care
No matter what the strife,
I'm born of Spirit, Calm and Joy
Born of Him, I'm born of Life.

The book of Acts talks about Saul (later Paul) who fervently persecuted the followers of Jesus until one day Jesus stopped him on the road to Damascus and chose him to be His own. In Acts 9:15, Paul is described by Jesus as "a chosen vessel to bear My name." This spoke to me in a deeply personal way and this poem describes how Jesus also chose me.

"For he is a chosen vessel of Mine to bear My name..." **Acts 9:15b (NKJ)**

His Chosen Vessel

He chose me; I belong to Him.
He lifted me from off the shelf
Of emptiness and all alone.
He said, "I have for you a home."
Then took me there unto Himself
And gently said, "You are My own."
His vessel.

He saw the dirt and every scar
From sin and hurt in other time.
He breathed His breath of Life on me,
Began to polish lovingly
And with each touch made light to shine,
"From this, my own, I set you free."
His vessel.

Then Living Waters He outpoured
And said, "Thus give I unto you;
This Joy of filling you may know
Til bursting with an overflow.
As I have done, now go and do,
This Life and Love to others show."
His chosen vessel.

In the book of John, Chapter 3, Jesus is teaching of Spirit and heavenly things, and in Verse 8, He compares the wind to the Spirit. From this came the poem "Windswept." I think of listing as leaning or bending down for Him to clean me up as a loving Parent.

The wind bloweth where it listeth, and thou hearest the sound thereof, but canst not tell whence it cometh, and whither it goeth; so is every one that is born of the Spirit. **John 3:8 (KJV)**

Windswept

The Spirit listeth where it may
To fill the wheat and blow the chaff away.

In quiet adoration do I stay and wait
Knowing that the One who comes will not be late,
That never is my Wind-swept life left up to fate.

Assured through tender union with Him every day
He shall in gentle leading take me His best way
So, I in stilled submission now can only say,

"Come, Holy Spirit, list to fill
And cleanse to bring me to Your perfect will."

These two poems, "Prayer" and "Time," I kept on the wall at work by the computer to remind me as often as needed to both redeem the time, and to always remember the true source of everything worthwhile.

See then that you walk circumspectly, not as fools but as wise, redeeming the time, because the days are evil. **Ephesians 5:15-16 (NKJ)**

❧ Prayer

Hello, God
Here am I,
Need
Reaching for
Supply.

Thank you, God
Here are You,
Love
Offering
To do

❧ Time

Time —
A friend
Holding my potential,
my maybes;
Whispering 'tomorrow,'
healing,
Keeping me walking
toward Hope.

Time —
An enemy
Stealing my memories,
my intentions.
Intoning 'history,'
fleeting,
Frittering away
the hours.

Time —
Impersonal
Except as I
give it Life;
Singing
or sighing with it,
Using it to produce
the Eternal.

In the book of John, Chapter 10, the Word tells me that Jesus, as my Good Shepherd, will speak to me and I will know His voice. This is a great promise and comfort to me.

And when He brings out His own sheep, He goes before them; and the sheep follow Him for they know His voice. **John 10:4 (NKJ)**

My sheep hear My voice, and I know them, and they follow Me. And I give them eternal Life, and they shall never perish; neither shall anyone snatch them out of My hand. ***John 10:27-28 (NKJ)***

Guided

"My sheep," said He, "shall know my voice."
Oh God, in this I do rejoice!
Great Shepherd, keeper of the lamb
Attune my ear to Thine "I Am;"
That I may hear You speak to me
And know the way to follow Thee.

That in each dark or lonely place
Though I may not see Your kind face
Your voice will tell me how to go.
For You have said — and it is so —
That God, though wandering I may be,
You promise to come after me.

Faithful to speak and show me how
To find Your constant path of now.
"They shall be guided by My voice."
Oh God, in this I do rejoice!

There are many pitfalls in life, I have found. In times of wayward straying, I have wandered into some. Still, I have known my Shepherd's voice as He has always spoken to me to return to the safety of His arms.

Hold Me

I'm prone to wander from you, Lord
Even though I love You
I long to do Your will
But it seems inside me still
There's a want to break away and go far from You.

I'm prone to wander from you, Lord
And go by my own choosing.
Oh, hold me to your breast
Where my fickle heart can rest
Don't let me go, don't let me be refusing.

I'm prone to wander from You, Lord
Though you are my dearest friend.
You know me way down deep
Yet in Your arms You let me sleep,
And You've promised You will keep me til the end.

I'm prone to wander from You, Lord
You knew it when You chose me
But so faithfully You've shown
That I am Your very own
And Your love just reaches round to enclose me
And oh, I thank You.

In the beginning of this journey with God, I was wary, wanting to protect my heart with doubt. This poem tries to express what happened when I said yes to the open invitation to trust enough to invite Jesus into my life.

Then you will call upon Me and go and pray to Me, and I will listen to you. And you will seek Me and find Me when you search for Me with all your heart. **Jeremiah 29:12-13** (NKJ)

Know Love

Ask it and ye shall receive,
Just test and let Me show you
Fullness never dreamed of
Come know Me as I know you,
Doubting child.

I slowly lifted wary eyes
To seek and really find?
Look quickly off — what cruel hoax,
What new trick of mankind?

And yet —
Just ask in solitary,
What could there be to lose?
No one need know I'm reaching,
Could there be choice to choose,
Hopeful child?

Oh, Savior if You're listening
Please hear me this one time.
Jesus come in, come into me.
Cleanse me and make me Thine
 Own child.

Ask it and ye shall receive,
Just test and let Me show you
Fullness never dreamed of
Come know me as I know you,

Brenda Wheaton Diffin

Trusting child.

As I reached out my hand to Him
And He reached out to me,
A miracle of change began
He gave new Life, new eyes to see
His Glory.

He lives, He loves, He touches!
And makes all things anew
His glow surrounds each moment
His promises all true
And you?

Could you but dare to ask Him
He'll show you that it's so.
You, too, can see the beauty
He yearns to help you grow
To know.

Ask it and ye shall receive
Just test and let Me show you
Fullness never dreamed of
Come know Me as I know you.
Know love.

Glimpses of Grace

The poem "Be Love" came from a longing and desire to share this new awakening to Life with others.

"This is my commandment, that you love one another as I have loved you." **John 15:12 (NKJ)**

Be Love

My Father, God, You've given me
This thrilling joy of being free
Free to enter into Thee
And take from You capacity
At once to live and love and be
All that You have planned.

How can this beauty be expressed?
How then to share with others lest
A child of Thine should go unblessed
Or unprepared to meet life's test?
How to convey the wondrous rest
From which Thine may stand?

Oh, let Your answer fill my ear
For You would have us without fear,
Assured that You will always hear
Faithfully waiting, gently near
To speak it softly, surely, clear.
Take me by the hand.

"My Word is Life, and ever true
And never child, could I fail you.
Express by Being what we two
United are and let Me do.
Keep clear the channel, Light shines through.
Love. Tis My command."

"On Flying" was written for a friend who was unsettled but searching for the truth of Being at Peace with Christ.

You will keep him in perfect peace, whose mind is stayed on You, because he trusts in You. **Isaiah 26:3 (NKJ)**

❧On Flying

Some of us for pleasure
Fly,
The joy-filled race of
Soaring — graceful
Free.

With some of us
It's fly we must;
Insistent echoes of
A lust
to See.

Still some there be
Who fly as fleeing
From ... as those
In storm, who search
A lee.

Of me and thee?
I sense the graceful
Freeing,
Expanse of seeing
And yes, the quiet lee.

Then ... so much more
Would you
Explore with me...   The Being.

In every life there are inevitable disappointments, losses, and times of grief. We who belong to God know He is with us. Still, our hearts cry out to Him for answers. These poems, "False Bravado" and "Truth", were written from one of those dark places. Questions and Answers; He hears us and does respond in the day of trouble.

I will call to you whenever I'm in trouble, and you will answer me. **Psalm 86:7 (NLT)**

❧ False Bravado

O, the lonely ache
Of "being strong"
O, the deep despair
Of "courage" shown;

The smile amid the storm,
Standing tall,
When feeling worn —
What does it take
To mend a heart
Severely torn?

And how much "doing
Of the next thing"
Can be borne?
When will the questions
Echo back
The answers known?

❧ Truth

But ask of Me
And I will be
The strength you need.

I'll be your smile,
I'll be the way,
And I will lead.

I'll be your balm,
I'll be your calm,
I am your creed.

I'll answer
any question
that you plead

And with it all
The love I give
Will more than feed

You — and yours,
And any — and all,
Who will but ask.

In the book of Jeremiah, God's Word tells us in Chapter 29, Verse 11, For I know the plans I have for you, says the Lord. They are plans for good and not for evil, to give you a future and a hope. (The Living Bible.) His Word is always active and living, and it inspired "A Plan."

A Plan

In everything there is a plan,
A time, a place, a reason.
Guided by His Holy Hand,
Touching all within the span
Of space and spore and season.

Touching me and touching you
With purpose, love, and care
Bringing Life to all we do
Meaning, hope and fullness, too
And giving us a joy to share.

One Christmas, I was just thinking about how the world sees the holiday and how different it is from the celebration of Jesus' birth — God's Son sent to Earth to be our Savior and Lord. This is "Why Christmas."

Behold a virgin shall be with child, and bear a Son, and they shall call His name Immanuel, which is translated, "God with us." **Matthew 1:23 (NKJ)**

❧ Why Christmas

If it were the pear tree
Or the partridge sitting there
Or the hens or geese or maidens; on and on,
The holiday could still be bright,
The music gay, the aura rare;
Lights would sparkle surely
And Santa's day would dawn.

Some faces would be glowing,
Our gifts might be the same.
The smells, the sounds, the busy bustle
Of tradition now unfolding
Done up with "good times" name
For the family and the loved ones
And the merchants' yearly hustle.

But, oh, there is a Something
That makes this glad time live
In the hearts of all He made one
in Jesus Christ our Savior,
The One who came to give
Abundant Life so freely,
The blessed Holy Son.

His Spirit is that something,
He sent the precious Dove
To make this day, the Christmas season,

Brenda Wheaton Diffin

And others all year through
Filled and overflowing with His love
He really cares, He loves you
And that alone His reason.

Glimpses of Grace

"Beside Still Waters" was written and sent as a Christmas Card along with a sketch of trees on the shore of Big Lake at the family summer camp in Maine.

He leads me beside the still waters. He restores my soul. **Psalm 23:2b-3 (NKJ)**

Beside Still Waters

Jesus —
He came upon this troubled earth
So very long ago

He came that He the Father's Love
To us might clearly show

That in our hearts this gift revealed
Might grow and daily fill

Til in all things we walk with Him
Beside the waters still.

I saw a photograph that moved me to think of creation, and light coming out of darkness. Jesus also being the Light of the World, and the Holy Spirit sent to us, upon Jesus' returning to the Father. I later painted the picture and was moved to write "Out of Darkness" based upon Holy Scripture.

Creation
When God began creating the heavens and the earth, the earth was at first a shapeless, chaotic mass, with the Spirit of God brooding over the dark vapors. Then God said, "Let there be light." And light appeared. And God was pleased with it and divided the light from the darkness. **Genesis 1:1-4 (TLB)**

Jesus
In the beginning was the Word, and the Word was with God, and the Word was God. **John 1:1 (NKJ)**

So, the Word became human and made his home among us. He was full of unfailing love and faithfulness. And we have seen His glory, the glory of the Father's one and only Son. **John 1:14 (NKJ)**

Holy Spirit
And I will ask the Father, and he will give you another Comforter and He will never leave you. He

is the Holy Spirit, who leads into all truth. The world cannot receive Him because it isn't looking for Him and doesn't recognize Him. But you know Him because He lives with you now and will be in you. **John 14:16-17 (NKJ)**

The Trinity
For there are Three who bear witness in heaven: the Father, the Word (Jesus), and the Holy Spirit; and these Three are One. **1 John 5:7 (NKJV)**

Brenda Wheaton Diffin

࿔Out of Darkness

Out of Darkness
Sterile, cold, echoing emptiness
Black and still in solid loneliness

Out of Darkness
 Burst a Word of wondrous holy love ***Creation***
Speaking, moving through with brilliant rays
Touching, sweeping, changing deadened ways
Spreading warmth in splendid radiation
Beauty beyond highest expectation

Out of Darkness
 Jesus, the Son of Almighty God ***Jesus***
Talking with mankind in tender tone
Showing us we need not be alone
Calling all in faith to turn from night
Freeing us by grace to walk aright

Out of Darkness
The Comforter - A promise fulfilled ***Holy Spirit***

Glimpses of Grace

Spirit of Truth, divine abiding
His perfect Light of Love residing
God expressed within in moments pure
Glowing, beaming forth, a beacon sure

Out of Darkness
Into the glory of Triune Love   ***Trinity***
Creator, Blessed Lamb, Heaven's Dove

"Inside Story" is from knowing the Truth of Life on the inside, but not speaking out due to shyness. A longing to share, and knowing if you could give it away, it would change a life, yet unable to express.

For you will be His witness to all men of what you have seen and heard. **Acts 22:15 (NKJ)**

Inside Story

Were you with me
… there inside,
Your eye to see
What shy would hide
…For just a moment,

You would concede
… walk away,
But that received
Today would stay
…With you forever

That tear I'd pay;
Companion cost of caring,
And not be grieved.

"Companionship" speaks of a lonely time, which surely, we have all experienced, yet not without hope in the form of our Christ and His Spirit of comfort.

Lo, I am with you always, even unto the end of the age. **Matthew 28:20 (NKJ)**

Companionship

What is life
That it should be so lonely?
In all that occurs
Within me stirs
Even strife —
If it replaces aloneness.

What is day
That it should be so solitary?
Moving forces talk
I sit and walk
My own way
And feel the separation.

What is night
That it should be so dark?
Shadows that appear
And stay so near
Without the light
Of companionship.

Who is Christ
Who dares to speak
A Word of hope
And throw a rope
To save me
And be my Comforter
What and
Who indeed?

This poem, "Don't Cry," reminds me again that if not abiding in Christ, I am "sorrow," but in Him there is promise of renewal, joy, and a safe harbor.

Come to Me all who are weary and heavy laden, and I will give you rest. **Matthew 11:28 (NKJ)**

I will both lie down in peace and sleep, for You alone, O Lord, make me dwell in safety. **Psalm 4:8 (NKJ)**

Wait on the Lord; Be of good courage, and He shall strengthen your heart; wait, I say, on the Lord! **Psalm 27:14 (NKJ)**

❦ Don't Cry

Gently blowing puffs of air
Seek to ease my mind
Have no worries, have no care
Whispers sweet and kind
Come to Me, my weary child
Your rest in Me you'll find.

Lift your eyes to heaven
Lift your heart and sing
Your days will not be even
But in My time, I'll bring
Days of comfort, times of joy
I'll ease your suffering.

Be patient child of sorrow
Your pain will make you strong
Take heart and on the morrow
To Me you'll still belong
I'll teach you worlds of beauty
You'll sing a lilting song.

Your heart will know the radiance
In others you now see
And yours will be the miracle
Of joining Me with thee
Take heart and dry your face now
Come trusting. Come to Me.

Elizabeth Barrett Browning wrote, "Earth's crammed with heaven. And every common bush afire with God." I thought of my beloved Maine and wrote "Reflections."

... The earth is full of the goodness of the Lord.
Psalm 35:15b (NKJ)

Reflections

Maine, home, myself
Waters reflecting past
Intensely private solitude
Soul-filling memories of
Strengths won through sorrows
But built on granite.

Maine, character, growth
Inseparable depths of being
Core of all that is
Love has triumphed
I am filled
God is everywhere.

Jesus is the Light of the World. And Jesus in me allows me to share the glorious Light of each day.

Then Jesus spoke to them again saying, "I am the Light of the world. He who follows Me shall not walk in darkness but have the Light of life." **John 8:12 (NKJ)**

Christ is Dawn

Dawn is having opened eyes
Awareness of a whole new realm
Urgent beckoning to come
Uncover darkness's disguise.

A Word, a touch, senses soar
All different now in seeing
Wonder in just Being
Rising eager to explore.

Being a single parent for a time pushed me ever closer to God to seek His wisdom in hard decisions. There are relationships that seem to be meant for a season, perhaps for a time of growth and trust. In Christ, we live in hope and possibility to perhaps grieve, but go on. I am humbled to acknowledge the incredible and unmerited kindness and grace of God in this area. He has shown compassion in every detail of my life as I have looked to Him. He does work all things together for the good of His people and for His glory. Even in these later years, I am so blessed.

Delight yourself in the Lord, and He will give you the desires of your heart. **Psalm 37:4 (NKJ)**

Hope deferred makes the heart sick, but longing fulfilled is a tree of Life. **Psalm 13:12 (NKJ)**

❧ Possibility

I thought the hurt of wondering
Was hard until I knew
That you
And I
Were through.

And then the hurt I knew
Was wonder…
In part,
That I had offered
You
My heart.

The wonder and the hurt I know
Must dim…
And then,
Because I am the way
I am…
Try again.   Maybe.

"Peace" was written at a time when our country was newly at war in the Middle East. It was sent, with a sketch, as a Christmas card to my family and friends — a reminder that our true source of Peace is always Jesus.

And the Peace of God, which surpasses all understanding, will guard your hearts and minds through Jesus Christ. **Philippians 4:7 (NKJ)**

Jesus Christ is the same yesterday, today and forever. **Hebrews 13:8 (NKJ)**

 Peace

Peace, oh Peace
Our heart cry.

Peace among
All men.

Jesus, God's reply
Jesus

Same now
As then.

Brenda Wheaton Diffin

My boundless appreciation to a new friend and sister in Christ, Beth Gooch, who picked up the challenge of putting this scattered work together in print. Her enthusiasm and encouragement have been inspiring and God-sent.

It is our hope that this modest body of work shows honor and gratitude to God the Father who has loved us from eternity past, God the Son who shows us what Love looks like in the flesh and died to guarantee our eternity future, and God the Spirit Who lives within and speaks to our hearts evermore of Himself as we go on.

Brenda Wheaton Diffin

www.ingramcontent.com/pod-product-compliance
Lightning Source LLC
Chambersburg PA
CBHW052123110526
44592CB00013B/1732